D0975529

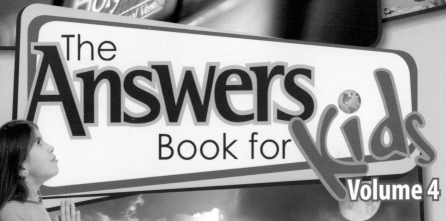

The Answers Book for Kids
Volume 4

22 Questions from Kids on Sin, Salvation, and the Christian Life

KEN HAM with Cindy Malott

Fourth Printing: February 2011

Master Books®
P.O. Box 726
Green Forest, AR 72638

Master Books® is a division of the New Leaf Publishing Group, Inc.

Printed in China

Book design by Terry White

ISBN 13: 978-0-89051-528-0
Library of Congress Control Number: 2009900146

All Scripture references are New King James Version unless otherwise noted.

Please visit our website for other great titles: www.masterbooks.net

When you see this icon, there will be related Scripture references
noted for parents to use in answering their children's, and even their
own, questions.

For Parents and Teachers

The fear of the LORD is the beginning of wisdom; and the knowledge of the Holy One is understanding (Proverbs 9:10).

Dear Moms and Dads:

Let's face it. Some questions are just more difficult to answer than others. Did Satan sin first? Why do animals die when they don't sin? Why do I get sick? Did God create the tsunami? What is heaven like? Did God create sin? Questions like these asked by our children today can leave us stumped.

It seems that after decades of studying the Bible, the more I know, the less I know! How can a book be so deep and rich in new wisdom and knowledge? It is a wonderful, blessed mystery that because His works are so great and His thoughts are so deep we will continue to learn about Him throughout all eternity (Psalm 92:5).

As we train up the children in our lives in the way they should go, we must remember to set the example of seeking answers in God's Word—even for the toughest of questions.

I pray that all the children who will be influenced by this book, will one day turn to the Bible to find the most important answer—the life-giving answer—that eternal life comes through belief, trust, and faith in Jesus Christ alone.

Ken Ham
President/CEO, Answers in Genesis

Question: Why did God create people when He knew they would sin?

Stephen P.

Age 10 — Toronto, Canada

4

Answer:

Oh, the depth of the riches both of the wisdom and knowledge of God! How unsearchable are His judgments and His ways past finding out! (Romans 11:33).

All things have been created by God to give Him glory. God is perfect and has complete knowledge of things past, present, and future. Everything He does is perfect. So, Stephen, how do I answer your question? Well, because we know God is perfect, we know that the entrance of sin into the world through Adam and Eve must have been a way to bring glory to God. But how could sin bring God glory? God is holy, hates sin, and the punishment for sin is death. Well, God had the wonderful plan to save sinners from eternal death through Jesus Christ. Jesus took the punishment for the sins of everyone who would believe in Him even though He had never committed a single sin. Jesus' amazing life, death, and Resurrection shows us how great God's love is for us. When we realize all that Jesus did so we could be saved, we want to shout for joy and give God all the glory! By creating Adam and Eve, God created beings to whom He could show His attributes — love, mercy, and so on. And think about it — by doing this, He has enabled us to exist and to be able to spend forever with our Creator!

Romans 11:36

5

Question:

Could God forgive our sins without the suffering of Christ?

Cheyenne

Age 9 — Belgium

6

Answer:

Nor is there salvation in any other: for there is no other name under heaven given among men, by which we must be saved (Acts 4:12).

Cheyenne, when we sin — when anyone sins — we are telling God, our Creator, that we don't want to obey Him anymore. Well, because He is our Creator, because He is holy and good, He must punish us when we sin. The punishment for sin is serious — eternal death and separation from God forever — unless we could offer a perfect sacrifice to God to pay for our sin. But we are NOT perfect. So, what do we do? Well, God had a plan. And it is a plan that provides a PERFECT sacrifice for you and me! That sacrifice was the Son of God; Jesus Christ. Jesus never did one single sin. He never lied, stole anything, or disobeyed His mother. In fact, He is the only person in the whole world who ever lived and did not sin! But He is the one who had to die for our sins. Our sin against God is so bad that it could only be paid for by Jesus Christ (the perfect One) suffering and dying in our place. Because of our sin in Adam, suffering was the consequence and in one man, Jesus, the full consequence was taken on our behalf. Jesus paid the price for our sin in full. Therefore, He suffered so that He could defeat suffering for all eternity for all who will believe.

When we trust Jesus and believe in Him, we can know that our sins are forgiven because Jesus Christ suffered for us and paid sin's penalty.

2 Corinthians 5:21; Romans 5:8

Question: Will God and Jesus keep me safe from Satan's fallen angels?

Nathan D.

Age 5 — Kentucky, USA

8

Answer:

For I am persuaded that neither death nor life, nor angels nor principalities nor powers, nor things present nor things to come, nor height nor depth, nor any other created thing, shall be able to separate us from the love of God which is in Christ Jesus our Lord (Romans 8:38–39).

It does seem like Satan and his angels might be able to do us harm, doesn't it, Nathan? And the Bible says that the devil prowls around like a roaring lion looking for us! We are told to flee from the devil — and we should do that when we know we are being tempted to do wrong things. Also, God promises His children, those who believe and trust in Jesus and live for Him, that He will never leave us. God's Word makes it clear in Romans 8 that when we trust in Christ, He is with us for eternity and no one can take that away from us. He is our helper and we should not fear! Sometimes, even though you know all of this is true, you still wonder, "What can I do when I still don't feel safe?" Well, bad things still happen on this earth, and God knew we might feel unsafe and scared. The Bible helps us with this, too! It tells us we must be prepared. We must put on the armor of God! No, it is not real metal armor, but something even better! It is the truth of His Word. Reading the Bible and having faith that what it says is true will keep us prepared for anything that happens here on earth. Because we will know that as His children, nothing will ever separate us from His love and one day we will spend all of eternity with Him in a perfect world.

1 Peter 5:8; Hebrews 13:5-6; Ephesians 6:10-18

9

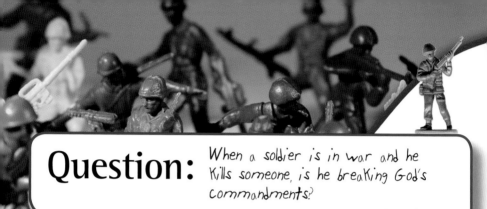

Question: When a soldier is in war and he kills someone, is he breaking God's commandments?

Sam W.

Age 8 — Texas, USA

Answer:

You shall not murder (Exodus 20:13).

Well, Sam, I think we need to take a very close look at God's commandment. See our verse? It actually says that we should not "murder." What the Bible teaches is that we should never kill another person (or even have hatred in our heart) because we're mad at them or jealous or just don't like them. Do you remember the very first murder? When Cain killed Abel? God knew that Cain was jealous of Abel, and that's why he killed him. We see in the Bible where God often instructed the Israelites to go to war in order to accomplish His purpose. Because of the sinfulness of man, God told the Israelites they had to fight against these rebellious people. This was a time of war — and very different from when there is hateful intention by someone and they take things into their own hands and kill (murder) someone. It is sad but true that as long as there is sin in the world, there will always be war. But keep in mind, when a soldier goes to war it is not "murder" because he is obeying his orders and defending himself against the enemy. He is not doing it to be hateful and he would stop fighting if the war was over.

Genesis 4:3-8; 1 Samuel 15:3

Question: When we go to heaven, we have to be perfect up there or wherever. Doesn't that mean our personalities will be changed and everyone will be the same?

Jaden W.

Age 12—North Dakota, USA

12

Answer:

And God will wipe away every tear from their eyes; there shall be no more death, nor sorrow, nor crying. There shall be no more pain, for the former things have passed away (Revelation 21:4).

Everyone will NOT be the same in heaven! We will be ourselves without sin! In other words, Jaden, you will never want to lie again . . . you will never have to worry about stuff being stolen . . . you will never be disobedient or selfish. But I believe each person will still be different from all the other people. I believe we will be different because when I look around the world and universe I see that our Creator (God!) LOVES variety. There are so many different, wonderful creatures, plants, stars, galaxies, and unique people. Also, there is a specific example in the Bible that helps answer your question. There was a time when Jesus went up a mountain with his friends, Peter, James, and John. While they were there, they saw Moses and the prophet Elijah . . . and they recognized them! That tells me that they must have looked different from each other — that Moses was still Moses and Elijah was still Elijah. And when Jesus showed Himself to people after He rose from the dead, He had a body, His disciples eventually recognized Him, but He was the same perfect Jesus. In heaven we will be individual people . . . that don't sin! It will be wonderful.

1 Corinthians 13:12; 1 John 3:2

13

Question: Why does God let the bad guys win sometimes?

Samuel P.

Age 9 — California, USA

14

Answer:

For indeed I am raising up the Chaldeans,
A bitter and hasty nation
Which marches through the breadth of the earth,
To possess dwelling places that are not theirs (Habakkuk 1: 6).

First of all, let's remember that when God created the universe it was all "very good." Bad things started happening when sin entered the world — after Adam chose to rebel and disobey God. Having said that, we need to also remember that God is all-powerful and all-knowing. Nothing surprises Him! He can do all things and no plan of His can be stopped! Look at our Bible verse above. In this instance, God used the bad guys (the Chaldeans). He ordered them to move, and He allowed them to win! It seems like a bad thing — but God NEVER does anything bad. God had a purpose then for the Israelites and the Chaldeans that would bring Him glory in the end. We can't see all that God sees. God knows exactly how everything will turn out. And in the end, God will judge all the "bad guys" (just as He eventually judged the Chaldeans), even though, from our limited human perspective, it seems they often win. In fact, the Bible says that we are all "bad guys" because we all sin against Him. And unless we are sorry for our "bad-guy ways" (sin) and trust and believe in Jesus Christ as our Savior, we too will face God's punishment.

Psalm 94:1-3; 1 Corinthians 15:24-25

15

Question: Why isn't Satan the first sin instead of Adam and Eve?

Ben F.

Age 7 — California, USA

Answer:

Therefore, just as through one man sin entered the world, and death through sin, and thus death spread to all men, because all sinned (Romans 5:12).

Sin actually entered the world through one man — Adam. Adam was God's special creation, the very first man. When Adam was created on day six, God said that he was to rule over all the earth and all that was on it. God also clearly told Adam not to eat of the fruit of the tree and if he ate he would surely die. Adam was the one who was given the instruction to obey what God said. So, because Adam was told to obey, and Adam chose to disobey God and eat the fruit, and Adam was given dominion to rule over the earth, Adam gets the blame for sin. Sin entered the world — to all of us — through Adam because we are his descendants. So, what about Satan? He was not the father of the human race (it was Adam), he had not been given dominion over all the earth (that was Adam, too), and so he is not the one responsible for sin in our world today. Adam's sin is considered the first sin . . . his is the sin that brought judgment on the human race and, in fact, on the entire creation. It is also important to understand that there is no way for Satan or fallen angels to have salvation. They have already been judged and thrown from heaven. Humans can have their sins forgiven. Therefore, the way God deals with humans is different from the way He deals with the angels.

Genesis 1:26; Genesis 2:16-17; Romans 8:22

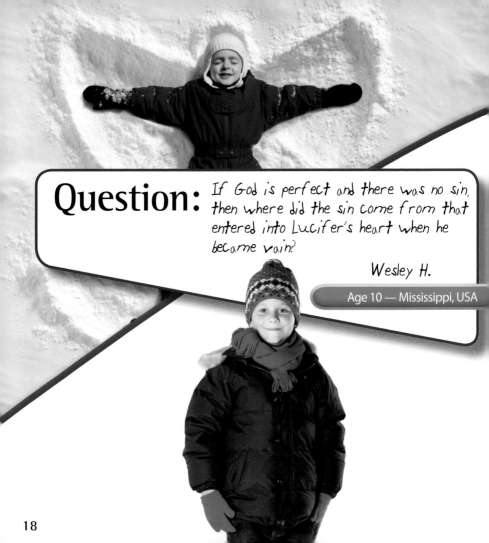

Question: If God is perfect and there was no sin, then where did the sin come from that entered into Lucifer's heart when he became vain?

Wesley H.

Age 10 — Mississippi, USA

18

Answer:

For by Him all things were created that are in heaven and that are on earth, visible and invisible, whether thrones or dominions or principalities or powers. All things were created through Him and for Him (Colossians 1:16).

God is perfect — we know that! Your question, Wesley, talks about Lucifer's sin and Lucifer's heart. This is where we need to be careful. Yes, the Bible tells us some things about Lucifer (Satan) and angels . . . but it is not a book about angels. God tells us in His Word that angels are created beings; they can never be like God. They are not all-powerful or all-knowing. Because they are not all-powerful, they can choose evil. Lucifer chose to turn away from God and became evil. He wanted Adam and Eve to turn away from God by disobeying Him, and Satan is still trying to get people to turn away from God today.

I believe that the sin and vanity in Lucifer's heart came when he chose evil over good and stopped glorifying the One who created him, the One who is all good and holy. Lucifer's rebellion was his own choice to turn against God. Because Adam listened to Satan instead of God, sin was brought into the creation. And please remember that although the Bible does tell us a little about angels, it is really a book about God and His wonderful plan to save people (like you and me) through Jesus Christ.

Jude 6; Genesis 3:1; John 17:3

Question: Why do animals die? We are the ones who sinned, so why are they punished? They didn't do anything wrong.

Samantha L.

Age 10 — Pennsylvania, USA

PRESIDIO OF SAN FRANCISCO
PET CEMETERY

GYPSY
1962 — 1976
THE CAT WHO

Answer:

For we know that the whole creation groans and labors with birth pangs together until now (Romans 8:22).

It is so very sad when an animal dies — especially a favorite pet. And you are right; they don't sin because they have no souls. But the Bible says that all things will die on earth because of Adam's sin in the Garden of Eden. Let me explain. If the principal at your school said there would be no recess, it affects everyone at your school because he is the head of your school, right? Well, God made Adam the head over the earth. He gave Adam "dominion" or power and control over the earth. Since Adam was our first leader, everything he did affected everything on earth. We know that God told Adam if he disobeyed he would surely die. So, since Adam had to die because of sin, everything on the earth would also have to die. And that includes all the animals. It wouldn't make sense to have sinful humans who would die when everything else around them remained perfect.

When our dog died, I was sad! But it reminded me how terrible sin is, and because of sin, everything and everyone must die. At the same time, I was joyfully reminded that because of Jesus Christ and His death on the Cross, the people who believe in Him would live forever with Him in heaven even though their bodies may die here on earth.

Romans 8:20-22

21

Question: If I am God's child, then why doesn't He keep me from being sick or hurt here on earth?

Jonathan S.

Age 10 — Kentucky, USA

Answer:

And God will wipe away every tear from their eyes; there shall be no more death, nor sorrow, nor crying. There shall be no more pain, for the former things have passed away (Revelation 21:4).

We often ask questions like: "Why am I sick?" "Why do people have to die?" "Why did my pet die?" Well, Jonathan, this is not the way God created the world to be. You see, after God created everything in the universe, He said it was all very good. If the world had stayed this way, nothing bad would ever have happened. But God created Adam with the ability to choose right and wrong. And even though Adam enjoyed everything in the Garden, and was even the head over all the earth, he still chose to do something terribly wrong. He chose to disobey God. Well, God made it clear that if Adam disobeyed Him by eating the fruit from the tree, then he would die. From that very first sin, all living things would have to die.

Sickness is part of dying. And even when you get sick and then get well again, it is still a reminder that the world is no longer "very good," the way God made it, because we all sin against Him. But there is great news! If you are God's child and believe in Jesus Christ, the Bible says there will one day be a place that is "very good" again; a place without the sickness and death that comes because of sin.

Genesis 1:31; 2:17; 3:6; Romans 8:22

Question:

If God can control anything, why did He let the tsunami hit and so many people get hurt? Did He create the tsunami?

Sam W.

Age 7 —Texas, USA

Answer:

And they feared exceedingly, and said to one another, "Who can this be, that even the wind and the sea obey Him" (Mark 4:41).

God does control everything that happens on earth and in the universe. He is the Creator of all. He can cause a tsunami and He can will that no tsunami come. But from the Book of Genesis we know that God created all things perfectly. Tsunamis, death, divorce, earthquakes, floods, fighting . . . all the bad things in the world . . . are because of sin. It's not God's fault these things happen — it is because of sin. Sin came into the world through Adam's choice to disobey God — we all sin because of Adam. When we sin, it is like telling God we don't want Him in our lives and that we prefer to do it our way. Terrible things in our lives show us what living without God — without His grace, mercy, and protection — may be like. But those terrible things also show us just how much we need Him!

Please remember, Sam, we are all sinners and sin is the most terrible thing in our lives. Because of our sin against God, bad things happen. It is so amazing that even though we don't deserve it, God sent Jesus who was punished in our place so that we could be forgiven. Those who believe in Jesus will one day live in a place where the bad things will finally be over for good!

Isaiah 45:7

25

Question: Why did Cain kill Abel?

Calista M.

Age 8 — New Hampshire, US

26

Answer:

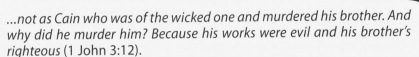

...not as Cain who was of the wicked one and murdered his brother. And why did he murder him? Because his works were evil and his brother's righteous (1 John 3:12).

We know that Cain killed Abel. If we look at the Bible account of Cain and Abel we see that they both offered sacrifices. But even though they both offered something to God, their hearts were different. You see, Cain's heart was wicked and evil. God warned Cain that sin would be "at his door" or that sin had a desire for him. This is a reminder to us that sin in our lives is always trying to persuade us to do bad things that dishonor God. This is what happened to Cain. Cain's sacrifice would not have pleased God because of that — no matter what it had been. Now, Abel's heart was faithful and true to God and his sacrifice was excellent in God's eyes. When Cain realized that God was not pleased with his sacrifice but accepted Abel's, his heart became more wicked. He was angry and jealous of his brother and killed him out of envy. Calista, when I read the account of Cain and Abel, I see that God knows our hearts very well. We need to pray that our hearts are pure toward God and when we serve Him, we do it because of the sincere love, honor, and respect we have for Him —not like Cain. Then He will be pleased.

Hebrews 11:4; Genesis 4:3-8

27

Question: What happens to the people who died before Jesus came? Are they in heaven or hell?

Adam S.

Age 8 — Hawaii, USA

Answer:

But you have come to Mount Zion and to the city of the living God, the heavenly Jerusalem, to an innumerable company of angels, to the general assembly and church of the firstborn who are registered in heaven, to God the Judge of all, to the spirits of just men made perfect (Hebrews 12:22–23).

Well Adam, Jesus is and has always been the central point of history. In the Old Testament, we read about the law that was given to the Israelites, and all the sacrifices they were commanded by God to carry out, all the festivals they were to keep, and all the feasts they were to conduct. The reason for all of these is that they pointed to Jesus. You see, since the Fall, when sin entered the world, everyone on earth through faith (either in Jesus who was to come or Jesus who has now come) has opportunity for salvation through faith. This is why the Jews had so many laws, festivals, and sacrifices, which now have all been fulfilled in Christ, the Messiah they were looking towards. It would have been impossible for a Jew to do something without it having reference to the Messiah yet to come. Praise God, the Messiah has now come. We all need to make sure we have put our faith and trust in Him.

So the point, Adam, is that people before Christ were saved by faith, and thus went to heaven when they died, and those who did not have faith were separated from God forever.

Hebrews 11:1-12:23, 13 Luke 16:19-25

Question: Did Adam and Eve go to heaven?

Danielle F.

Age 10 — Canada

30

Answer:

By faith Abel offered to God a more excellent sacrifice than Cain, through which he obtained witness that he was righteous, God testifying of his gifts; and through it he being dead still speaks (Hebrews 11:4).

Well, Danielle, the Bible doesn't say for sure if Adam and Eve went to heaven or believed God's promise of the coming Savior. I think that the Bible shows that it is a good possibility. Look at our verse above from the great faith chapter of Hebrews. God tells us that Abel offered an excellent sacrifice to God, that he had faith, and that he was made righteous. Abel was Adam and Eve's son and it seems that the only way he could have learned about God was from his parents. After all, they walked with God and talked with God. They were the first two humans ever created. They were the first to sin and that sin started the practice of making sacrifices to God for the forgiveness of sins. (Remember how God killed an animal to make clothes for Adam and Eve because they suddenly knew they were naked?) Abel knew how to offer a sacrifice that was pleasing to God. He offered that with a heart that believed in God through faith, and he probably learned that from his parents, Adam and Eve. If all that is true, then it seems as though Adam and Eve knew the truth as well, and if they did, they will be in heaven.

Genesis 2:18; 3:8; 3:21

HOLY BIBLE

Question: What is heaven like? Are there really mansions? Will I stay ten forever?

Chelsea G.

Age 10 — Virginia, USA

32

Answer:

In My Father's house are many mansions; if it were not so, I would have told you. I go to prepare a place for you. And if I go and prepare a place for you, I will come again and receive you to Myself; that where I am, there you may be also (John 14:2–3).

My dad used to tell me that heaven is where God is and sin is not. In heaven we will see God's glory and worship Him with the angels and heavenly creatures. The Bible refers to mansions in our Father's house. Will there really be mansions? It could be. But whatever Jesus is referring to here, we know that it will be something amazing that our minds can't even imagine. But the most important thing is that Jesus will be there. We know it will be an awesome, beautiful place and really BIG! Unlike anything we have ever seen before! And what about your age? What kind of body will you have? That is not made clear. Let me tell you what the Bible DOES say. The apostle Paul describes the body as a tent. Something that will be destroyed when we die (when our souls go to be with the Lord.) And the Bible tells us that one day we will have new physical bodies that will be different from the bodies we have now. What will the changes be? We don't know for sure. I truly believe it will be something like Jesus' resurrection body!

Matthew 6:9; 2 Peter 3:13; Revelation 21:16-27; 1 Corinthians 15:51-52

33

Question: How will I know what to do when I get to heaven?

Leah E.

Age 6 — Ohio, USA

34

Answer:

But as it is written: "Eye has not seen, nor ear heard, Nor have entered into the heart of man The things which God has prepared for those who love Him" (1 Corinthians 2:9).

We can't even begin to imagine what heaven will be like and to actually be in the presence of our wonderful God! The Bible tells us that there will be no more crying, no more death, or sorrow, or pain. Everything will be made new, and right, and perfect! Leah, it is a wonderful place God promises for us. But, it is only for those who know, trust, and believe in Jesus Christ our Savior. When you trust in Jesus, believe He died on the Cross for you, and tell Him you are truly sorry for your sins, He will forgive you. That is the only way any of us will ever get to heaven. And here is the important thing Leah — we should not want to get to heaven because we think it is a cool place for us! No, we want to be in heaven because we love God and want to worship Him. Do you know what the people are doing who are already in heaven? The Bible tells us they are glorifying and worshiping God. When we get to heaven we will have perfect love for God and He will be our primary and eternal desire. We will worship Him in full happiness and will never want to stop. That is the day that we should all look for.

Revelation 21:4-5; Psalm 16:11

35

Question: What does being "born again" mean?

Kyle R.

Age 6 — Illinois, USA

36

Answer:

Jesus answered and said to him, "Most assuredly, I say to you, unless one is born again, he cannot see the kingdom of God" (John 3:3).

A long time ago, a Jewish ruler (Nicodemus) came to Jesus and asked the very same question. He wondered how in the world a person could be born again when they were already old. Jesus' answer was very clear. Being born again means becoming part of God's family — the word "again" literally means "from above" — becoming a child of God. This is different than being born like a baby is born; this birth is a spiritual birth. It is something that happens in our heart. It is actually becoming a new creation. Let me explain. When I was born again into God's family, my life changed and my heart changed. I knew I was God's child now. The things I wanted to do were different. I wanted to learn about God. I learned to trust Jesus and understood that without Him I could never get to heaven. I wanted to go to church and learn more about what the Bible says. I began to love God more and more (as I got to know Him better). I learned that God hated my sins, but that if I was sorry for them and if I believed that Jesus died on the Cross so I could be forgiven, then God would forgive me. Being born again has given me assurance that I will one day be in heaven with God, my Lord and Savior! It can do the same for you.

John 1:12; 2 Corinthians 5:17; Romans 10:13

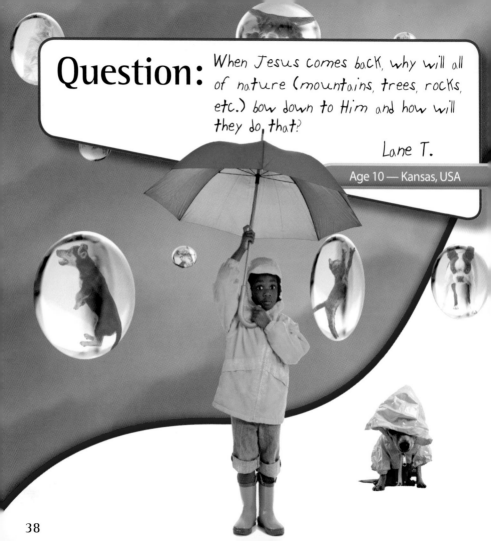

Question: When Jesus comes back, why will all of nature (mountains, trees, rocks, etc.) bow down to Him and how will they do that?

Lane T.

Age 10 — Kansas, USA

Answer:

For you shall go out with joy,
And be led out with peace;
The mountains and the hills
Shall break forth into singing before you,
And all the trees of the field shall clap their hands (Isaiah 55:12).

Lane, the Bible actually contains 66 different books. It contains different styles of writing. For instance, we know the Book of Genesis is history and tells us exactly what God did. But there are other books, like the Psalms, that are considered poetry. Now poetry is different from history. Poetry can use different words to describe things. When you hear someone say, "It's raining cats and dogs," do you really think that cats and dogs are coming out of the sky? No, it is just the way we talk to describe something we might have a hard time describing otherwise. So when God tells us that the mountains and the hills will cry out and the trees will clap their hands, God is describing joy and delight and praise that is really too great to even imagine. He is saying that people will be filled with joy and will be celebrating! As you continue to study the Bible, you will see that in spite of different styles of writing and the use of some figures of speech, God always conveys His message perfectly.

Proverbs 30:5; Psalm 19:8

Question: Why did Jesus preach in the Middle East and not America?

Joy B.

Age 11 — Michigan, USA

40

Answer:

Go therefore and make disciples of all the nations, baptizing them in the name of the Father and of the Son and of the Holy Spirit (Matthew 28:19).

When Jesus came to earth, He knew exactly what He had to do. He had a ministry and a plan. Jesus wasn't preaching very long before He called his 12 disciples to join Him. Jesus' message to the people was that He was God and that He was the promised Savior, the one who would save the people from their sins. Jesus preached to the people but also taught His 12 disciples in a special way. After three short years, Jesus was crucified. But before He died, He told His disciples He would send them a Helper (the Holy Spirit) — and He said to go into all the world and preach the gospel. His plan is for people to take the gospel throughout the world. The Helper would give wisdom and courage to continue teaching in Jesus' name. They did receive that wisdom and courage and continued to share the good news about Jesus. They taught more and more people . . . and those people taught more people . . . and Christianity spread to many nations. So the answer to your question really is that although Jesus only preached in the Middle East, His word is still spreading today as He commanded to happen. The Apostles — the word means "messengers" — took the gospel to the rest of the world because Jesus commanded to take it to Jerusalem, Judea, Samaria, and to the ends of the earth. So the message of salvation came from Jesus, and He commanded it should be spread to the whole planet.

Mark 16:15; Acts 1:8

Question: Did God cry when Jesus died?

Cheyenne

Age 9 — Belgium

Answer:

Jesus wept (John 11:35).

The Bible tells us that Jesus wept. He wept at the grave of His friend, Lazarus, and He wept as He drew near the city of Jerusalem for the last time. We know that Jesus is God — that He became a man, was crucified, rose from the dead, and went back to heaven. So when Jesus cried, this was God crying — but it was God in His human form crying. Thus, Cheyenne, we know God has emotions. Now, when Jesus died it was different. Jesus cried to God the Father, "Why have you forsaken me?" At that moment God the Father turned His back on the Son because of our sin. This was always part of God's plan to offer a perfect sacrifice to save those who would believe in Jesus. So was God crying when Jesus died? Well we don't know — but I'm sure He was more sad than we could ever be. Even though it was terrible, God knew that Jesus' obedience to Him on the cross would bring Him glory. God knew that it would complete His plan for eternal life in heaven to anyone who would believe in Jesus and trust Him for forgiveness and salvation.

John 10:30; 11:32–34; 17:3, 5; Luke 19:41; Isaiah 53:10

Question: If Satan changed everything by tricking Eve, how do I know Jesus can keep me safe from him?

Nathan D.

Age 5 — Kentucky, USA

Answer:

You are of God, little children, and have overcome them, because He who is in you is greater than he who is in the world (1 John 4:4).

Well it wasn't Satan who changed everything — really, it was our sin in Adam that changed everything. When God created Adam and Eve, He didn't make them to be like puppets. He wanted them to enjoy Him, obey Him, and love Him. But we know that Adam and Eve didn't do that. Satan tempted Adam to sin (even though God created him with the ability not to sin). When Jesus was on earth, Satan tempted Him also, but Jesus resisted and overcame Satan, thus sealing his doom. Because of Adam's sin, we all sin (remember Adam was the first human created and God made him the head of the human race) and because we come from him, what he did (sin), we did. We too deserve to be punished for our sin. But don't forget God's wonderful plan of salvation which He had worked out before He created the universe! God wanted to show us how much He loved us by sending His only Son to earth, that whoever believes in Him will share eternal life with Him in heaven! You'll still need to watch out for Satan. He is always trying to get us to disobey God. You can help stop Satan's influence in your life by reading your Bible, believing it, and praying for God's wisdom. Whenever you do sin, tell God you are sorry — as a Christian, your sin has already been forgiven, but we need to learn to be like Jesus every day. When we let God know how sorry we are for our sin, that even helps us recognize the sin problem in our own life !

Romans 3:23; 6:23; John 3:16;
Ephesians 1:13; 1 Peter 5:8

Question: How do we know other religions aren't true?

James

Age 9 — Ohio, USA

46

Answer:

Nor is there salvation in any other, for there is no other name under heaven given among men by which we must be saved (Acts 4:12).

No religion other than Christianity has a book like the Bible that tells us about the origin of everything, and who we are, where we came from, what our problem is (sin), and what the solution to our sin problem is. No other religion has a Savior who is alive (He rose from the dead). All other religions require people to do something to work out their future — only Christianity has the solution that we can't save ourselves, only God can do it. So how can we know if other religions aren't true? Well, if they don't agree with the Bible they are not true! There are two main tests I want you to use though. First of all, any religion that claims to be true MUST believe that Jesus is God! Remember, Jesus Himself told us that He and the Father are one. Many religions talk about God a lot . . . but if they don't believe in Jesus and that He is God, and they don't believe that Jesus' death on the cross and His Resurrection results in our sin being forgiven if we will receive it, then it is not the truth! The other test is to find out if they believe that salvation is given to those who trust in Jesus . There is nothing you can do to save yourself. We could never do enough good works to get us to heaven, but Jesus did it when He died for us! Jesus Christ is the way, the truth, and the life.

John 10:30; 14:6; Ephesians 2:8-9

47

Answers Are Always Important!

The Answers Book for Kids answers questions from children around the world in this four-volume series. Each volume will answer 22 questions in a friendly and readable style appropriate for children 6–12 years old; and each covers a unique topic including, *Creation and the Fall; Dinosaurs and the Flood of Noah; God and the Bible;* and *Sin, Salvation, and the Christian Life.* Explore:

- Why the first person God created was a boy.
- How Adam named all the animals.
- Why the Bible is true.
- What being "born again" means.

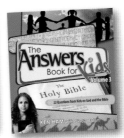